The Hottest Business Income Opportunities...

...for the '90s

Table of Contents

Introduction

The '90s are well upon us, and the trends that have governed business in the '80s have shifted to a more conservative school of thought. Gone is the Trump era, where great fortunes in short periods of time were sought after, with the int ention to buy everything in the universe and turn it into some kind of marketable product. No longer are would-be entrepreneurs investing millions of dollars in plans and schemes and promises of enormous wealth with little or no effort. What has not changed, however, are indications that more and more people are taking their financial future into their own hands, and turning toward self-employment and business ownership as ways to beat the threats of recession and establish for themselves and their families a secure financial base.

With an increasing threat of economic stress, it is becoming more and more difficult for the entrepreneur to find businesses that offer all of the security benefits as well as financial benefits that they are looking for. Never before has there been a directory that lists the best business opportunities for the '90s, detailing only businesses that will survive the current shift in entrepreneurial thinking. The entrepreneur who is in tune with these trends will be able to cash in during this decade.

DIRECT MARKETING

Few businesses in the '90s exhibit the same potential as direct marketing. Direct marketing is simply the selling of something by mail. There are several things that you can sell, but the most important thing to remember is to take the time to research your product. In doing so, you will ensure your investment. You will be able to make accurate predictions as far as how your product will sell, and how much you should charge. Try to find a product that fills a particular need. One entrepreneur started on his way to financial security during a time of economic recession. During the mid-'70s gas crisis, he simply sold the plans for a still that would make alcohol for automotive use. His advertisement said that he could help people fuel their cars for about 10 cents per gallon. This generated enough interest that 18 months after he stopped running the ad, he was still getting orders in the mail. How would you like to fuel your car for 10 cents per gallon? Are there any other needs that you can see need to be filled? How about selling survival equipment? Isn't that something that is on people's minds right now? What else could you sell? Do you have an interest or hobby that is shared by other people? How would you like to make money with your hobby? Imagine the following scenario.

Just before dawn you step out of your truck. You note that the ground is frozen. You will be silent, but your quarry will be even more subtle. You smile inwardly. It will be a great hunt.

The mountain slopes away from you to the west. Sunlight streams through canyons the to the east, but where you are, it is dark. High on your tree stand, you will be in a shadow long after the sun has risen.

You picked this spot on a trip over Labor Day weekend. It is just as you remembered: surrounded on three sides by trees, bordered on a fourth by a slow-moving stream. This time of the year, the grass is yellowed and bent with the weight of the early-morning frost.

The evidence of whitetail is everywhere. By the water, there are several tracks pushed into the frozen earth, and by the edge of the clearing, matted grass where the buck has lain to watch his herd. The trail is well worn, and shows signs of recent use. The deer will come. Of this you are sure.

But will they come before you have to go home to get ready for work? And when they do come, can you trust your old Browning to bring them down? You look at your watch. Just how much time **do** you have? Maybe a couple of hours this morning, all day Saturday, and if you can work it in, a few more hours here and there. All told, you have little more than a day and a half to spend hunting. Why? Because you have to work to support your family.

Your mind turns to another question. **Why** are you still using the old Browning? As you sit in your tree, you ponder this mystery. By the time you buy a few boxes of .273's, gas for your Landcruiser (which is as old as your rifle), a hunting license, and a thermos of hot coffee, you are broke. How are you going to be able to afford all that next year, **and** a new rifle? You shake your head, and wait. If there was just a way to have enough time to hunt, and afford a new rifle, too . . .

THERE IS!

Through direct marketing, you can have the time and the resources you need to be able to enjoy hunting or fishing whenever you want. Imagine having enough time to stay out for as long as it takes to bag your deer. Imagine walking into a gunshop knowing you have enough money to buy a new Weatherby .416, several hundred boxes of shells, enough gas for your 10 days of hunting, and enough left over to pay the mortgage.

What else can you think of that might sell? 1990 will be remembered as the year that Saddam Hussein of Iraq invaded Kuwait. Many people have taken advantage of this incident to secure their financial future.

There was a company that was selling Saddam Hussein T-shirts. There was a group of people that were offering to send hate mail to Saddam. Some other people cashed in on the military presence in Saudi Arabia by selling military patches associated with Operation Desert Shield. Still others sold what amounted to propaganda, both supporting and detracting from the US military presence in the Middle East.

There will be other world incidents that you may be able to cash in on. Do you remember the Fall of the Wall? Many people caught up in the spirit of celebrating the liberation of East Germany found that they were able to realize huge profits in direct marketing by offering everything from T-shirts to pieces of the infamous wall through direct marketing. Even today, you can still look in magazines and find Wall memorabilia. In fact, there is a company that has just minted commemorative coins celebrating the event and is offering them through direct marketing.

One of the most successful products you could ever hope to find for your direct marketing business is information. Are you an expert in some area? Do you have a degree or other experience that sets you apart in some area or another? Many entrepreneurs are finding that information is the ideal product, because the return on information is often 10 times that of the investment. In this age of information exchange, valid, valuable information is quite a commodity for which people will gladly pay you. In the '90s, so much information will be exchanged that there is no way that information consumers will be able to keep up without using some kind of information resource.

Take this book that you are using. Obviously, you are seeking specific information on what businesses are "hot" for the '90s. Do you have time to go out and conduct surveys of all the businesses in your area, conduct tests of economic conditions, and inform yourself of market trends that will affect your business? Unless you are blessed (or cursed) with extraordinary amounts of time, you won't have the time to find out all the things that you will have to take into account before you decide what businesses are going to be successful in the '90s. An information broker, however, makes a living of finding out information that is important to you, and to thousands of others like you who need the information, but do not have the resources to obtain it on their own. People will pay you for information that is important to them, and they will pay you for your expertise. In the next chapter we will discuss a great way to market information.

Direct marketing is such a versatile business because it is so adaptive to almost any situation. People have been able to cash in on everything from economic crises to current fads. You can too.

YOUR OWN 1-900 NUMBER

The 900 number is one of the most potentially profitable business ventures ever devised by man. With a 900 number, you have at your disposal one of the most powerful tools ever invented for the purpose of distributing information. At this stage of world history, accurate, relevant, and important information is at a premium. The best way to cash in on the information revolution is to operate your own information service, and the best information service currently is the 900 number.

The possibilities before you are limited only by your imagination. If you have a line on a particular piece of information, there is a good chance that there is a market for it. In other words, there are people out there waiting to pay YOU for your information.

So, how do you get a line on a particular bit of information? It's easy. Simple research is your best bet. Any piece of information has a source. All you have to do is tap into that source. Because the calls are limited in length, you will not have to explain in great detail a particular piece of information. All you have to do is find things that are worth reporting (and repeating) that can be covered in three to five minutes. This pamphlet will give you a few ideas, but don't let yourself be limited by the suggestions given here. You can adapt these ideas to suit your own needs, or you can invent your own!

Description of Service

There are several different types of 1-900 numbers available to the information provider. You will find that different companies offer different options such as length of call, total line capacity, interactive calling, and direct billing. You can also opt to rent a line, rather than purchase one, which will save you quite a bit of initial investment, though you will have to assign some of your profits to the owner of the line for rental. Some offer a basic rental of one line. The lines can be rented on a weekly basis, with no minimum length of time. Generally, however, you must let them know 30 days in advance if you want a termination of your service. Some lines can handle 1,000 or more calls at one time. Each caller will hear your entire message. For an additional cost of $2,500, you can opt for interactive calling. This will allow your customers to press a number on their telephone to obtain specific information. For example, if you are providing a recipe sharing service, you can include on your initial message a brief sentence such as, "If you would like dessert recipes, press number one on your touch tone phone. If you would like entree recipes, press number two. If you would like information on how you can sell your own recipes, press number three." The cost of such a service is greater than that of a line with no interactive calling, but the returns are higher, as each customer spends more time on the phone.

Important Information

As you establish yourself in the Information Provider business, there are several things that you should know in order to enhance your chances of success.

First, you are not required to have a business license; however, the

FCC is required to know exactly what information you are providing.

Some things that have been successful for other information providers, such as Dial-a-Porn and credit repair information, will put you at a great legal risk if you are not conscientious about your adherence to regulations. Because the owner of your line is legally responsible to the Federal Communications Commission for the information provided on lines provided by us, oftentimes they cannot allow the following information:

• adult programming

• information oriented toward young children (such as Santa Claus and Easter Bunny)

• credit repair

• sports scores or gambling odds

• information pertaining to criminal activities (how-to info for car stereo thieves etc.)

Finding Information

As with any product, you must find a market for the information that you would like to cater to. Keep your ears open. What are people talking about? What do people say they would like to know? Have you ever heard somebody say "I wish I knew more about tax laws"? How many times have you wanted to know what the weather would be like at your favorite water-skiing lake on a given day? People buy magazines that update the goings on in their favorite soap. Why wouldn't those people call YOU to find out the same information, for roughly the same price, from the convenience of their own home? The fact is, people are more than willing to pay for information, and if that information is convenient to obtain, they will pay even more. And what is more convenient than the telephone?

Look around you. Ask your friends what they would like to know. Ask them what information they would be willing to pay for to find out. Try to attune yourself to the information needs of the people around you. Chances are, those needs will be more or less universal.

Adapting Your Information

Once you have decided what information you are going to distribute, you will need to format that information so that it can be conveyed clearly in the time allotted. There are several things you will need to do to before you sell the information.

Break the Information Down

Take the information you have and pick out the key elements. Maybe not all of the information is relevant or important. It is up to you to decide what parts of the information you have you are going to sell. For example, if you have a list of 5,000 cars that can be bought below wholesale, and you know that in three minutes, you can only give information on three cars, you will have to choose the three cars that you feel will be of most interest to your callers. Make sure that the information that you do give is relevant and important so that your caller doesn't feel that you are wasting his time and money.

Use Telegraphic Language

When someone calls to find out what the weather will be like for their weekend camping trip, they don't want to hear statements like "Saturday's forecast is brilliant, warm sunshine with a few fluffy, drifting, vaporous clouds swimming lazily in a deep ocean of sky, with a minute, ever-so-slight chance of electrical disturbance, with chances of cold, acidic precipitation increasing significantly by the sabbath day." This may be an extreme example, but the point is that the camper only wants to hear "Mostly sunny Saturday, with an increasing chance of rain Sunday." Don't try to use flowery language to make your presentation longer. The caller will recognize what you are doing, and will recognize that he is paying for every second. The risk to your credibility is not worth the few extra cents you will squeeze out of your callers. Make sure that you only give them the information that they are paying you for.

Because the calls are limited in length, try to stick to the fundamentals of the information you are providing.

DISTRESSED MERCHANDISE

Do you have a fax machine? Do you have access to a fax machine? Does someone you know have access to a fax machine? If you answer yes to any of these questions, you can cash in on one of the greatest opportunities for the '90s. In keeping with the trend of rapid information exchange, through a service called FONE, you can cash in on information about distressed merchandise that you can purchase at prices far below wholesale, and then turn around and sell to retailers, or even offer them to corporations in your area as business incentives or premiums. Usually this information is sent to retailers first, but through the FONE service you will get this same information, often before retailers find out about the offering.

All manufacturers have times when they want to sell merchandise as quickly as possible. In cases like these, most companies are willing to let products go at extremely low prices. This is a source of low-cost products that can be sold elsewhere. Those who can tap into this source of merchandise can make a lot of money doing so.

When merchants have closeout merchandise available, the only ones who generally find out are standard retailers. That is because the routes of communication are usually the same as the routes of distribution. Small stores and consumers never hear about these closeout bargains. The best deals are offered to large wholesalers or retailers who buy frequently from the manufacturer. These dealers usually add a heavy markup to the price and are still able to offer it as a sale item. The discounted items, which the retailer may have purchased for 10 percent of retail value, bring in customers when they are marked up to 50 percent of the suggested price.

Until recently, consumers had no access to this closeout network. However, there is now a way for you to buy current name-brand merchandise for far below what most wholesalers pay. That is possible because of the FONE (Fax Opportunity Network Exchange) system, which has recently become available to everyone with a fax machine. The FONE system is an information network that makes this type of bargain available to you.

Getting started with FONE is easy. There are a few things you need to do to prepare yourself to make the most of FONE, but this course will guide you through them. There is no reason for anyone to give up and say it is too hard.

Access to a Fax Machine

First, of course, you must have access to a facsimile (fax) machine. Fax machines are wonderful inventions because they allow the rapid, easy transmission of written material. Fax machines are also very convenient: Even if you are not near the fax machine, it can still receive messages from FONE, and you can use the information on the fax message whenever you have the time. The technology of fax machines is what makes FONE possible.

Fortunately, having access to a fax machine may not be as difficult or as expensive as you think. If you choose to buy a fax, you can find one for a very low price, and those prices are going down every day. If you do not want to or cannot afford to buy your own machine, you still have a number of ways to receive FONE information. If your place of employment has a fax, you may be able to receive messages on that machine. Maybe you have a friend who has a fax machine. Or you can rent a fax mailbox from the companies that have these services. However you decide to do it, getting a fax is not nearly as difficult as it used to be.

Entrepreneurial Spirit

You will also need a desire to make money and some creative ideas. Selling the merchandise you buy over the FONE network will take ideas and determination, but this course will also help you with ideas. In fact, the entire second section of this course is devoted to ideas for selling merchandise. If you feel like you don't have many ideas, that section will get you started on more possibilities than you could pursue. You can pick the ones you like and act on them. FONE merchandise is of high quality, and the low prices naturally attract buyers. This course will show you how to simply turn this to your advantage, using available avenues to market goods you find on FONE.

Contacts

Another thing you should do is think of potential contacts you may have. Specifically, you should try to cultivate contacts that will provide you with distribution channels. These channels could be anything you want; since the FONE merchandise is so inexpensive, there are an infinite number of possible ways to sell it at a profit. Your job is to find some ways to distribute the material. Later in this course, you will learn some proven methods of selling material you have bought through using the FONE system.

You should also be able to recognize a good deal when you see it. All the deals that come over the FONE system will be good ones for someone, but they may not be ideal for your situation. You should be able take a look at all the offerings that come over the FONE system and then decide which ones are for you. If you have no way of getting rid of discounted wristwatches, you probably should not order any, unless you plan to wear them yourself. You should also be able to determine how much of a good thing is best for you. For example, there may be 10,000 baseball mitts offered at 15 cents on the dollar, but you should be able to look at that amount and say, "I have the capability to sell 150 of these mitts." If you buy too many, you could have a problem on your hands. A healthy dose of common sense will help you take maximum advantage of the opportunities FONE will give you.

Making Time

You will also need another commodity that is somewhat rare among many people — time. FONE will not require a lot of your time, but it is not something you can neglect. As an FONE subscriber, you will be looking for ways to distribute bargain merchandise. It will take some creativity and perseverance. The market is definitely out there, but it will take you time to find it and tap it. Therefore, to succeed through FONE, you should have (or be able to make) at least a little spare time each week.

Making time is something that everyone can do — especially if there is a lot of money involved, as there is in this case. You may want to organize your time a little more carefully than you do now. If it is necessary, cut out one television show each week or wake up a few minutes earlier each morning. You **can** make time, and it will be worth it once you have your FONE business going.

If you have the things described in these paragraphs — access to a fax machine, an entrepreneurial spirit and creative ideas, possible contacts, the ability to see a good deal, and a little bit of time — you are ready to start making money through the FONE system. If not, you can get most of them rather quickly. You probably already have a fax machine, but if you don't, they are certainly within your reach. Prices are falling almost monthly, and you can get an adequate machine for about $300-$400 at this writing. Chances are you have an entrepreneurial spirit, too, or you wouldn't have had an interest in FONE to begin with. Most people have some contacts as well. If you don't believe you have contacts, you should think again. A contact can be anyone from a relative to a neighbor to a boss to an old classmate. Anyone who likes bargains is a potential customer. Of course, contacts who have a way to market discount merchandise are especially valuable. But just because you don't know anyone who owns a supermarket chain doesn't mean you don't have a market for discount goods. In fact, later in this course you will learn how to turn regular, everyday contacts into profitable avenues for selling merchandise. If you can tell a good deal when you see one and you can make a little time, you are ready to make big money by using the FONE system!

How FONE works

FONE gets its information from the source — the manufacturer. In fact, FONE gets the exact information that is given to ordinary retailers. But FONE gets it first. Because FONE has forged business links with manufacturers over the last few decades, it has become possible for FONE to get information most people cannot get. And you can get that information, because FONE distributes it over a fax network that spans the entire United States. By joining this network, you will join a small group of people who know where the truly spectacular bargains are to be found.

FONE acts as a conduit in two ways. First, it provides you with information about inexpensive merchandise that is available. FONE sends information on these opportunities as soon as it arrives, and moments later you will receive it on your fax. You will know the exact price and amount of the items available, and you will receive a detailed description of the offering. In many cases, you will get a facsimile of a page from a catalog or sales brochure that describes the item. Therefore, when you get information from the FONE service, you will know everything you need to know to buy quality merchandise at bargain prices.

Second, FONE provides you with an easy way to purchase that merchandise. You are also provided with an order form that allows you to order the merchandise via your fax machine. The order forms that you have received can be photocopied and used to order the items that you have chosen to purchase.

What Kinds of Merchandise Does FONE Offer?

FONE offers all kinds of merchandise. Past offerings over the FONE network include baby grandfather clocks, curtain material, crystal glasses, belts, hydraulic equipment, baseball gloves and other sporting equipment, luggage, gas pump gloves, wristwatch radios, outdoor furniture, and watches — to name only a few.

FONE also anticipates that in the future, more and more buying opportunities will come about as the FONE system expands and gains buying power. This will occur as more and more subscribers add their names to the network. The opportunities are only expected to get better, and there is no reason to suppose that opportunities will diminish as more subscribers join the FONE network. They should actually increase.

Each of the items offered over FONE has been quality merchandise made by well-known companies. Many so-called discounters sell poor quality merchandise, but that is not the case with FONE. FONE deals in only high quality, well-known items. In the past, for example, FONE has sold merchandise made by Samsonite, Bulova, Spalding and Coleman. These items have a high perceived value, and you can use that perceived value to make money. Customers who would be suspicious of a $55 baseball glove that cost only $11 will accept the glove as legitimate if it is a Spalding glove and you can show them the most recent Spalding catalog to prove it. Not only would their suspicions be allayed, but they would also want to know how many they were allowed to buy and when they could get them!

Why is the Merchandise so Inexpensive?

Some FONE customers wonder how FONE can get merchandise at such low prices. There are a few answers to this question. Since not all cases are the same, there is no one answer that can explain all the bargains. Many different factors account for the availability of quality merchandise at below-wholesale prices.

First, many items are simply being cleared out to make room for other models. The changes between models can be very simple; often only a minor characteristic such as color is altered, and because an item is blue instead of red, it is sold at 1/10th of the normal retail value.

In one recent case, a large, well-known company decided to change the color of its two-gallon coolers. Therefore, the company decided to let the old coolers go for less than 50 cents. The coolers normally sold for about five dollars. FONE offered more than 100,000 of these coolers over its network. Many FONE subscribers bought and resold these coolers, but not all were purchased before the information went to retailers. Later, these discontinued coolers appeared in a national drug store for about three dollars. The drug store chain used the low price on coolers to bring in customers anxious to get a good deal. In the process, the retailer made a lot of money on each unit. This type of profit margin is not uncommon.

Another reason merchandise appears at cut-rate prices on FONE is business closings. Often when a business closes, it needs to get rid of excess inventory fast. This is especially true when a bankruptcy or loan foreclosure is involved. By knowing that a certain company is trying to liquidate everything, you can find information about buys that will provide you with high income opportunities.

Overproduction is another cause of FONE bargains. Sometimes companies will produce a large amount of merchandise, then find themselves overstocked. In order to free up warehouse space and cut their losses, these companies will practically give the material away to be rid of it. If you can find a buyer for such overproduced merchandise, the potential for profit is enormous.

There are a number of other miscellaneous causes for FONE bargains. For example, labor or transportation difficulties can sometimes crop up and make it difficult for a manufacturer to sell products as it had expected. In cases like these, many companies are willing to sell their inventories cheaply and quickly rather than risk further delay. Also, some companies who are introducing a new product to the market are willing to sell a certain amount of that product cheaply in order to get it into people's hands and get some word-of-mouth advertising. If you become a middleman in this type of advertising distribution, you only have to add a small amount to the price of each item to make a lot of money.

You may have realized that in most of these cases, **time** is the key factor. When a company has introduced a new model, it wants to get that new model out as quickly as possible, so it is willing to make room by selling items at a low price. When a business is closing, creditors usually demand the remaining inventory be sold as soon as possible. The best way to do that is to lower prices. When a company is saddled with overproduction, it wants to quickly free the warehouse space and get rid of excess inventory. That time consideration drives down price. Similarly, when companies have labor problems or logistical problems, they want to get rid of these problems as soon as possible. Also, if a company wants to achieve a high customer recognition of its product, it wants to get those bargain-priced items into customer's hands as soon as possible. Time makes all the difference in discount merchandise. FONE is specially designed to take care of that need. Because they are electronically connected to a central information network, FONE users are able to get to this competitively priced merchandise before retailers and other buyers. The most important element of off-price buying — time — is on the side of FONE users.

Why Does FONE Have Access to This Information?

FONE has a number of connections that allow access to timely information that can save you money. These connections are the reason FONE can offer you such great bargains. The sources of FONE data are people who have had business links with large manufacturers for many years. These manufacturers are willing to release closeout information on the FONE system because it offers promise of selling the merchandise quickly, and that is the manufacturer's primary objective. If FONE subscribers do not use the information given, the manufacturer can then give it to retailers, who are usually eager to have such bargains.

Obviously, manufacturers and distributors do not ordinarily sell to the public. There are established lines of distribution that are limited by customary business practice. However, FONE has established links that an average consumer could not ordinarily get access to. FONE is the only real accessible source of these connections, and therefore, FONE subscribers enjoy an immeasurable advantage over anyone they compete with — including retailers, who normally add substantial markups to the closeout merchandise they purchase and resell.

The information you will receive as an FONE subscriber varies widely. FONE is able to get valuable closeout information from a number of businesses because FONE has been able to establish business links with all these companies. That means that when you get information from FONE, you will have access to much more than one line of products. As mentioned before, the types of merchandise available are diverse and growing.

CONSULTANT

Direct marketing isn't the only way to perpetuate the exchange of information. If you have expertise or experience in a field, you can rest assured that there are people who will pay you for the experience and expertise that you have. There are many things that you can do to share your knowledge. As has already been mentioned, you can share the information that you have through direct mail. You can also set up a consulting business that you can run at home or in an office building.

Look around you. Is there some kind of information that you have that others have expressed that they would like to have also? Are you a stock broker? Do you have stock information that helps you decide how and when to invest? Do you know someone who is a stock broker? Many times, you can cash in on the knowledge and experience of others.

Do you have any other information that people are interested in? Take a look at your interests. Are you a model builder? If so, have you gained any insights or tips on helping people enjoy the hobby of modeling? Are you an outdoorsman? Do you have information that other outdoor enthusiasts would be interested in, such as places to hike, or places to find equipment and training? Anything that you can do to perpetuate information will almost certainly be profitable as a business in the '90s.

There is some information, however, that has proven to be sought after by thousands and thousands of people. One such area is that of education. With recent cutbacks in government spending on education, students (and their parents) are looking more and more to privately offered scholarships and other sources of financial aid. There are so many scholarships offered that there is no possible way that the average student can know all of the financial aid that he qualifies for.

Ideally, parents start saving for their children's college education from the time the children are born, but unfortunately we do not live in an ideal world. Most parents do not start thinking about financing college until their child's junior or senior year in high school. Others start saving earlier, but the wrong way. Because of their savings, they won't get the financial aid they might have gotten otherwise. In addition, many parents find it necessary to use the equity from their homes to finance college expenses, making their house payments higher as they move closer to retirement and old age.

College is expensive. All you need to do is pick up a newspaper or listen to the TV or radio to hear of the rising college costs. Or better yet, just ask a parent who has a child in college. The college years can be the most financially draining years for both the parents and the student.

Currently, college costs for Ivy League schools run around $24,000 per year; private colleges cost around $16,000; and state- owned schools are between $6,000 and $8.5 thousand per year. In addition, the costs quoted by the individual colleges may not be accurate. They may not have included all of the expenses such as transportation or room and board. Even when the figures are accurate, the cost of college will vary individually depending upon the personal expenses involved such as food, clothing, and entertainment.

College cost are constantly on the rise. Between 1989 and 1990 alone, costs rose 7-9 percent, and college costs continue to rise each year. The year 1989 marked the ninth year in a row that college costs rose higher than inflation. In fact, Opinion Research Corporation found that 82 percent of the general public agree that rising college costs will soon make college an unreachable goal for most people.

Many parents turn to need-based federal aid programs to come up with the needed funds. Unfortunately, there have been drastic budget cuts in many federal aid programs. And what financial aid is still available runs into snags when people fill out the forms incorrectly. The Association of Fund Raising Council found that 80 percent of the applications for financial aid were misdirected or not filled out properly. For example, one mistake many people make is incorrectly stating the value of their home, thus lowering their eligibility for financial aid.

Other applications for need-based government aid are rejected because the applicants do not know how to present the case for their need to its best advantage. For example, some people can defer their income to the next year, thus lowering their yearly income. And the lower a family's income, the greater their financial aid eligibility.

Federal aid is not the only money available to college students. Scholarships are another option. However, many of the well-known scholarships are highly competitive, making it harder for the average student — or even the above-average student — to get a scholarship.

Because of these snags, many parents and students become discouraged, especially those with incomes between $30,000 and $75,000 per year. But that does not have to be the case. There are scholarships and other sources of financial aid out there that few people know about. And you can help people find the money they need to continue their education.

When looking in educational trade publications, college newspapers and other education publications, you will find scholarship services that offer to find all of the aid that a student might qualify for. These services are becoming more and more common, but there are still far too few to meet the needs of the students. University attendance is on the rise and will continue to rise, as will the cost of education throughout this decade.

Another trend of the '90s is that people are less and less in control of the demands that are placed on their time. Many of today's professionals are not able to meet all the demands of their time, simply because their time is mismanaged. Some companies have been able to cash in on this particular trend, as has been seen by such products as the day planner and all of the paraphernalia that one can purchase to increase management efficiency. You too can secure a financial future by offering executives and other professionals methods that they can utilize to increase their time management efficiency.

These tips can also be used by students, housewives, and any other person who finds that he is unable to adequately meet the demands that are made on his time. Time management is a valuable resource that will stand you in good stead during the '90s, if you are able to harness the power of time management and show others how they can also.

This business has all of the appeal of things that you should take into consideration while choosing a successful business for the '90s. By applying a few simple techniques, you can teach yourself and others how they can literally add hours of usable time to their days. You can incorporate this business into a consulting business, a service business, or even a direct mail business by offering cassettes and instructional materials that will help people manage their time.

SERVICE BUSINESSES

No matter what the economy, services are always needed, and you will find that a service business has much more stability and potential for success than a product-oriented business, because a service business is much less dependent on economic conditions and the mentality of the consuming public.

As a prospective business owner, you have before you the unique opportunity to fill a need, to provide a service that people want and are willing to pay for. There are literally thousands of things that you can do!

Most people, when they are toying with the idea of going into business for themselves, find that they are more inclined to start a business that will utilize the skills or talents that they already possess. It would be much easier to start a health-care service if you are already trained as a physician or other health- care professional, such as a nurse, than it would be if you were a mason or plumber by trade. You may also find that you will have more success if you start a business that is in line with your interests. One of the appeals of working for yourself is doing a job that you enjoy rather than just working for a paycheck. Your interest in your work will also affect your commitment level.

Evaluating Your Resources

What resources do you have at your disposal? How much money do

you have to start? What can you do with that money? What support
equipment do you already have? What will you have to purchase? What
training do you have? What skills have you acquired? What are your
interests?

In order to accurately evaluate your preparedness to enter into
business ownership, you need to be able to answer all these questions.

What Are Your Resources?

Look around you. If you are going to start a house-cleaning
operation, what things do you have already? Look in your garage. You
may find old rags and brushes that you just haven't gotten around to
throwing out yet. Among those rags and brushes, you may find valuable
tools to help you get on your way to building an inventory of products
that you will not have to purchase, at least not until you have already
established your business.

What things do your friends have? Maybe you know someone who
just bought a new vacuum cleaner. Offer to buy their old one (as long
as it is still in reasonable condition). Don't let an opportunity to save
money pass you by just because you don't want to use second-hand tools.
Anything you can do to lower your overhead will go a long way toward
increased profits.

How Much Money Do You Have to Have to Start?

Many people mistakenly feel that starting a business is impossible because of the costs involved. That is a myth. There are hundreds of thousands of things you can do that can cost as little as a few dollars. A service business in most cases lends itself especially well to minimal investment. You are not obligated to put up large amounts of capital to fund the production of a particular product. Basically, you are selling your time and your expertise, which generally can command a much higher price than a product can.

What Can You Do With That Money?

As you evaluate the resources you have at your disposal, you will need to decide just how you are going to make use of them. For example, if you have one thousand dollars to invest in your company, what exactly are you going to do with that money? Making a budget is the only way that you will be able to accurately gauge the outflow of your capital. A budget will allow you to monitor your expenses and will allow you to plan for the needs that will arise.

What Support Equipment Do You Already Have?

There are several things you can do to beat the costs of starting your new business. Making the most of resources that are available to you is probably the best way. If you are starting a house-cleaning or apartment-preparation service, chances are you already own a vacuum cleaner, even if its just your personal unit. If it cleans your home, why can't it clean another?

At the outset, you probably will not have so many clients that you will have to purchase an industrial or heavy-duty unit. This can save you several hundred dollars that you can allocate to another area of your budget, such as advertising. Look around your house. What other items do you already own that can be converted or otherwise put to use for your company? Anything that you can do to cut your overhead cost will have a positive effect on your profit margin.

What Will You Have to Purchase?

You may find in your garage or attic many things that you can use to start your business, but more than likely there will still be several things that you will have to purchase. It is important to know exactly what things are required, and which of those things you already have, so you can have an accurate idea of what you will need to purchase. Many times, service businesses require little in the way of support equipment. You may even find that there really is nothing that you will have to pay out for, except maybe advertising costs. However, if there is anything that you need to purchase, it is a good idea to know well ahead of time so you can fit it into your budget.

What Training Do You Have?

Many times, people who have gone into business for themselves have started businesses that they have worked in previously (for someone else!). They find that they are able to apply to their venture the training that they have received elsewhere. The skills and training that you have acquired working for someone else may turn into some of your most valuable assets as you are starting your business.

Other people have found that they have spent several thousand dollars for an education, only to find that there are no jobs available in their area of study. Rather than let all the time and money that they spent in acquiring an education go to waste, they take the skills they have and create their own business.

What Are Your Interests?

As we mentioned earlier, your commitment level to your business will be greatly influenced by your interest in it. Many people cite the reason for starting their own business in the first place is to be able to do something that they enjoy. You may find that a hobby could be a profitable business. How would you like to be paid to do something that you enjoy, or that you have even paid other people so you could do it in the past?

Evaluating Your Abilities

As you sit down to evaluate your resources, you should also take into account your abilities. Usually, as you are starting a business, if you stay within your abilities (a general composition of your skills and interests) you will have more success.

A music recording engineer in the Intermountain West decided to open his own studio. At the time, he had little training in the recording business; most of his expertise coming from recording his own music at studios. With little regard for the necessity of learning all that he could about the recording industry, he purchased the equipment he thought he needed and opened his doors for business.

He is now well established, but by his own admission, his learning of the industry came from, as he puts it, ". . . a matter of being embarrassed in front of our first few clients." This is not a positive way to approach your new business. This individual succeeded because of his inordinate musical ability, certainly not because of his extensive knowledge of the recording industry.

You can significantly increase the chances of your success by keeping within the limits of your abilities. Fortunately, most people have acquired some skill or ability that others will be willing to pay for.

Service Ideas

Are you beginning to get a clearer picture of what you can do? Hopefully by this time you have at least an idea of what direction you would like to pursue. Starting is simply a matter of taking the first step: choosing a service.

By this time, you should have a good grasp of your abilities and interests. Now your task is to find a service that matches your interests and abilities.

Included in this course are workbooks dealing with the possibilities of three services: a janitorial service, a housecleaning service, and an apartment-preparation service. Do not limit your thinking to these ideas unless you have already decided that these are the types of businesses that you would like to go into.

Listed below are 50 service business ideas. These are given with the intent to help you get started thinking about the right business for you. You are the only person in the world who can determine what that business is.

- alarm installation service
- apartment-preparation service
- appraisal service
- auto detailing
- carpet cleaning service
- ceiling cleaning
- child care service
- chimney sweeping
- clothing repair
- collection service
- consulting service
- coupon mailer service
- dating service
- delivery service
- dog breeding service
- dog training service
- event planning
- home inspection service
- housecleaning
- house painting
- house sitting
- hunting/fishing guide service
- information broker
- ironing service
- janitorial service
- lawn care service
- laundry service
- maid service

- mailbox service
- mail sorting service
- mobile bookkeeping service
- personal shopping service
- pet sitting service
- photography service
- pool cleaning service
- private mailbox service
- recipe exchange
- recyclables collection
- resume writing
- taxi service
- temporary help service
- tutoring service
- typing service
- vehicle broker service
- video taping service
- vinyl repair service
- wedding planning
- window washing
- windshield repair service
- writing service

These 50 ideas are not random choices, but have been carefully selected to meet certain guidelines. For example, none of these businesses will require special licenses for you as an owner, other than the normal city, county, and state business licenses. All of these businesses can be started and operated by one person. However, all of these businesses lend themselves very well to expansion. The most appealing feature of this list is the fact that all of these businesses can be started for less than $10,000.

You may find that one or more of these businesses would be interesting to you. You will also find that you can adapt these ideas to fit your own needs. If one of these businesses does not fit into your frame of skills abilities and interests, perhaps a variation will suit you better. If for some reason none of these are feasible, at least you will have a better idea of your limitations.

Whatever you decide to do, adaptation will be a critical element of your success. Generally you will find that you need to be flexible in all areas of your business. Eventually your business will settle into the most profitable and most comfortable niche. In other words, you will need to adapt your service to the market. It is impossible to fit the market to your service.

As you are deciding on a business, you should ask yourself several questions:

- Can you identify and plan the business you are planning on establishing?

- Have you identified your business service?

- Do you have an advantage over your competitors?

- Can you identify your competitors?

- Can you exploit the advantages you have?

- Is there a demand for your service?

In a later chapter on drafting a business plan, we will explain how to answer these questions.

As you evaluate your resources, including your skills, interests, and financial preparedness, you may want to consult with local business people and experts in your area who can provide valuable insight as to growth potential, and matching your resources with the local market needs. This will dramatically increase your chances of success.

CONCLUSION

No matter what you decide to do, there are several questions that you need to satisfy before you decide on a business for the '90s. First of all, you should ask yourself how the business will fare during times of economic recession, a real threat of the '90s. You should then try to determine what market trends are taking place that will affect how your product or service is received. Try to anticipate where those trends are heading, and try to stay ahead of them so that you are always on the leading edge of business in the '90s.

Much more so than the '80s, the '90s are turning out to be a decade where people are more interested in security, rather than quick and easy wealth. You will do better to steer away from the risky investments and opportunities that brought much wealth to people in the '80s. Though this is a more conservative era, you will be able to secure the financial future that you have always wanted by paying attention to all the factors that are changing that will have an effect on your product or service.

The American Dream is alive and well, and it is the courage and efforts of entrepreneurs such as yourself that will keep that dream alive and preserve the great heritage of free enterprise that our country has enjoyed for hundreds of years. Good luck in your venture, and enjoy building a secure financial future for you and your family.

COURSES AVAILABLE

for your convenience

Cashing in on Direct Marketing . . . .$ 399

Owning Your Own 1-900 Number . . . .$ 595
This includes 1 line of your own

FONE . . . . $ 499
Fax Opportunity Network Exchange

College Scholarship Service . . . .$ 595

Home-based Businesses for the '90s . . . . $ 299

ORDER FORM

Name_____

Address _____

City_____ State_____ ZIP_____

Phone (   ) _____

Enclosed is my payment of $_____
☐ Check enclosed

Please charge my credit card
☐ VISA   ☐ Master Card   ☐ American Express   ☐ Discover

Account # _____ Exp. Date _____

Signature _____

Send to: **Amercian Business Seminars • 1700 South 75 East • Provo, UT • 84606**